Little Fawna
is Loved, Safe, And Never Alone...

Ipek Williamson

"Little Fawna shines the light of optimism and hope into the life of any child who reads it. We need more children's books like this, although few will be as good."
~ Steve Chandler, Author of *Reinventing Yourself.*

Published by Limitless Insights Publishing, February, 2022
ISBN: 9781778065507

Copyright © 2022 by Ipek Williamson

All rights reserved. No part of this publication may be reproduced, stored in or introduced into a retrieval system, or transmitted, in any form, or by any means (electronic, mechanical, photocopying, recording or otherwise) without the prior written permission of the publisher. This book is sold subject to the condition that it shall not, by way of trade or otherwise, be lent, resold, hired out, or otherwise circulated without the publisher's prior consent in any form of binding or cover other than that in which it is published and without a similar condition including this condition being imposed on the subsequent purchaser.

Typeset: Greg Salisbury "Red Tuque Books"
Book Cover Design: Greg Salisbury "Red Tuque Books"

DISCLAIMER: This book is a work of fiction. Names, characters, places or incidents are either the product of the author's imagination or are used fictitiously. Any resemblance to actual persons, living or dead, events, or locales is entirely coincidental. Readers of this publication agree that neither Jo De Rosa nor her publisher will be held responsible or liable for damages that may be alleged or resulting directly or indirectly from the reading of this publication.

Dedicated to my husband Craig, our sons, Connor, Ali, Colm, and all the innocent children of the world.

One day, Little Fawna found herself in the middle of nowhere. She didn't know how she came there and where all her family and friends went.

They were there a minute ago, and while she was admiring the water trickling down through the rocks, they were all gone.

She felt frightened at first, thinking they had abandoned her. And she asked herself, "How will I find my way back to where I belong? How am I going to find my mom?"

She closed her eyes and took a few deep breaths that helped her calm down. Her heart wasn't racing anymore after a few breaths. She felt calmer. Then she opened her eyes and started to look around her.

First, Little Fawna saw a rabbit. She watched him enjoying the fresh and crisp clovers. She thought, "He must be hungry. Eating so fast."

The rabbit looked at her and said, "Hello, little fawn. What a beautiful day, isn't it?" Fawna answered, "Hello to you too. And yes, *it is* a beautiful day."

Then she noticed a beautiful red bird and listened to his song. He must have been calling his partner as another bird joined him quickly. They started to sing together and jump from branch to branch playfully.

They waived at Little Fawna and received back a big smile from her. She asked them where their nest was.

They showed her a comfy nest placed higher on the tree, where Little Fawna noticed the baby birds looking down, smiling at them.

She then saw the little pond a few steps ahead. She decided to drink some water. And when she got closer, she noticed the fish swimming calmly in the crystal-clear pond.

She said "Hi" to the fish while quenching her thirst with cool and fresh water. They responded saying, "Hi there, little fawn. How are you today?"

She said, "I am well, thank you. Waiting for my mom to come and find me." One of them said, "I'm sure she will very soon."

These quick and warm connections with the rabbit, the birds and the fish made her feel safe. She realized that she wasn't alone after all and surrounded by goodness and beauty.

She continued chatting with her new friend. And soon enough, she heard a familiar voice behind her. Little Fawna turned around to find her mom looking at her, smiling and relieved.

She introduced her mom to her friends. Her mom thanked the rabbit, birds and the fish for keeping Little Fawna company while she looked for her.

Little Fawna promised her newly found friends that she'd come back and visit with them again.

Left with her mom, thinking what she learned from this little adventure today, "Even when we think we are all alone, there's always someone willing to be there for us, and help."

"Does it mean we are never alone? I think it does..."

We are never alone... *You*, are never alone...

CPSIA information can be obtained
at www.ICGtesting.com
Printed in the USA
LVHW070559160222
711262LV00002B/63